ICONS
OF
STYLE

DENIM

MITCHELL BEAZLEY

DENIM

The
**DAILY
STREET**

Contents

The world of denim is steeped in history and innovation. The further you dig into the topic, the more you begin to understand the impact denim has had and why it has managed to build a cult following. It's a source of seemingly endless fascination to the fashion and textiles fan, as well as those interested in cultural movements.

With this in mind, writing a book on some of the most iconic denim to have impacted style isn't as black and white as some of the other topics in our *Icons of Style* series. Some jeans have had a huge effect on style purely due to their innovations in the most basic of forms, such as the addition of belt loops in 1922 (can you imagine jeans without belt loops these days?). Others have had an effect thanks to those who wore them, often on the big screen, such as Hollywood icons James Dean and Marilyn Monroe. Some brands and styles made a huge impact and then vanished from pop-culture memory, such as Rifle Jeans and the acid-wash craze of the 1980s. Regardless of what they did or why they have been featured in this book, all of the denim moments you will find in the pages that follow have played an important role in the story of denim so far.

It's a story that is rich in innovation, experimentation and even revolution, and, as old as denim is, we still can't get enough of it. Some people regard the denim jean as the most important creation in fashion history to date, and by the end of this book you should, we hope, be able to understand why they feel that

Introduction

way. From mineshafts to catwalks, from dance floors to billboards, denim has infiltrated every level of society and culture across the globe and it continues to do so.

Our taste for denim and its varying price tag fluctuates over the years, but it never dies. In the 1970s and 1980s designer denim boomed thanks to Calvin Klein, creating a whole new market for the material and opening it up to a new audience. It was a market that continued to do well throughout the 1990s, helping to change the general perceptions of denim and denim products as the indigo seeped further into popular culture. By the late 2000s our love affair with highly priced designer denim would subside, mainly thanks to the economic crisis, but it's a market that is rising once again. One side effect of the recession was that we turned our attention back to quality and value for money, something that can easily be distinguished in good denim.

For those who are well versed in denim history and culture, there will be several familiar names in this book, but, we hope, with a few surprise entries and facts along the way as well. For those who love their jeans but have yet to begin the long dig into the history of the topic, this book should be an eye-opener and a great place to start on your journey to becoming a denim specialist.

No. 139,121

J. W. DAVIS.
Fastening Pocket-Openings.
Patented May 20, 1873.

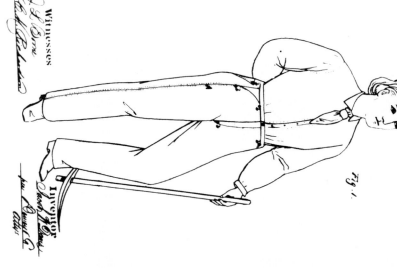

Fig. 1.

Witnesses

Inventor

UNITED STATES PATENT OFFICE.

JACOB W. DAVIS, OF RENO, NEVADA, ASSIGNOR TO HIMSELF AND LEVI STRAUSS & COMPANY, OF SAN FRANCISCO, CALIFORNIA.

IMPROVEMENT IN FASTENING POCKET-OPENINGS.

Specification forming part of Letters Patent No. 139,121, dated May 20, 1873; application filed August 9, 1872.

To all whom it may concern:

Be it known that I, JACOB W. DAVIS, of Reno, county of Washoe and State of Nevada, have invented an Improvement in Fastening Seams; and I do hereby declare the following description and accompanying drawing are sufficient to enable any person skilled in the art or science to which it most nearly appertains to make and use my said invention or improvement without further invention or experiment.

My invention relates to a fastening for pocket-openings, whereby the sewed seams are prevented from ripping or starting from frequent pressure or strain thereon; and it is contained in the employment of a metal rivet or eyelet at each edge of the pocket-opening, to prevent the ripping of the seam at those points. The rivet or eyelet is so fastened in the seam as to bind the two parts of cloth which the seam unites together, so that it shall prevent the strain or pressure from coming upon the thread with which the seam is sewed.

In order to more fully illustrate and explain my invention, reference is had to the accompanying drawing, in which my invention is represented as applied to the pockets of a pair of pants.

Figure 1 is a view of my invention as applied to pants.

A is the side seam in a pair of pants, drawn in, or colored, as traveling upward, which terminates at the pocket; and B B represent the rivets at each edge of the pocket-opening. The seams are usually ripped or started by the placing of the hands in the pockets and the consequent pressure or strain upon them. To strengthen this part I employ a rivet, eyelet, or other equivalent metal stud, b, which I pass through a hole at the end of the seam, so as to bind the two parts of cloth together, and then head the two parts of cloth together, which already have one head are used, it is only necessary to head the opposite end, and the work can be performed by this means I avoid a large amount of trouble in mending portions of seams which are subjected to constant strain.

I am aware that rivets have been used for securing seams in shoes, as shown in the patents to Geo. Houghton, No. 64,015, April 23, 1867, and to I. E. Washburn, No. 123,313, January 30, 1872; and hence I do not claim, broadly, fastening of seams by means of rivets.

Having thus described my invention, what I claim as new, and desire to secure by Letters Patent, is—

As a new article of manufacture, a pair of pantaloons having the pocket-openings secured at each edge by means of rivets, or substantially in the manner described and shown, whereby the seams at the points named are prevented from ripping, as set forth.

In witness whereof I hereunto set my hand and seal.

JACOB W. DAVIS. [L. s.]

Witnesses:
JAMES C. HAGERMAN,
W. BERGMAN.

Although denim had already been around for hundreds of years, it was a singular moment in 1873 that created the denim jean as we know it today. Rewind to 1853, when the Bavarian-born Levi Strauss founded his dry-goods business called Levi Strauss & Co., aimed at cashing in on the Gold Rush in San Francisco. As successful a businessman as Strauss was, he owed a great deal to a man named Jacob Davis, a tailor from Nevada who created the copper-riveted workwear for which the brand would become world famous.

The partnership between Strauss and Davis created its first products in 1872: riveted workwear made from either cotton duck or true blue denim. However, it wasn't until the following year, on 20 May 1873, that Levi Strauss & Co. and Jacob Davis received patent #139,121 from the US Patent and Trademark Office on the process of riveting denim waist coveralls – officially marking the creation of the blue jean or, as it was called then, the 'XX'. The name was a reference to the best ('extra, extra strong') denim manufactured by the Amoskeag Manufacturing Company of Manchester, New Hampshire, where the original jeans were made.

Opposite: The story of the blue jean starts here, with US patent #139,121. Below: Workers stand proudly outside the original Levi Strauss & Co. in the 1890s.

Levi's 'XX' – birth of the blue jean

1873

BLUE EYES
MINE

A lesser-known part of the early history of Levi's is the 'Nevada' jean. One of the earliest designs from Levi Strauss & Co., this jean was subsequently nicknamed the 'Nevada' after a pair dating from between 1880 and 1885 was discovered at the bottom of a mineshaft in Nevada in 1998, put up for auction on eBay on 24 May 2001, and purchased by Levi Strauss & Co. Archives for $46,532. Research by Mike Harris has even suggested that the 'Nevada' could actually be a predecessor to the 'XX'.

The Levi's 'Nevada' looked very much like any early Levi Strauss & Co. jean, with a single back pocket, a selvage waistband, crotch rivet, a cinch and suspender buttons. The 'Nevada' also included a unique 'knife' pocket on the rear outer of the left leg. As these jeans were created before the invention of the double-stitch sewing machine, the distinctive arcuate (bow-shaped) stitching on the rear pocket will have been stitched twice using a hand-mechanized, single-stitch machine, giving it a charming character.

In 2001 Levi's Vintage Clothing reproduced the 'Nevada' jean to celebrate its return to the company, painstakingly replicating the shape and distressing of the original. The LVC team in Europe studied the original pair in order to best replicate the fit, fabric construction, labelling, rivets and buttons, with the manufacturing taking place by hand at its Valencia Street premises in San Francisco, then the oldest existing Levi Strauss & Co. factory (built in 1906). With only 501 pairs created, these limited-edition replicas have become a sought-after collector's item.

Opposite: Two miners pose outside a mine in 1882. Miners were some of the earliest adopters of Levi's jeans, back when they were designed solely as workwear.

Levi's 'Nevada'

1880

Early Levi Strauss 13
& Co. advertising
played on
the product's
strengths (literally,
in the form of the
rivets), depicting
scenarios that
the clothing was
designed for.
This advert is
from the 1880s.

In 1886 Levi Strauss & Co. added one of the most iconic elements to its jeans – the Two Horse logo, branded on a leather patch sewn on to the waistband. Aware that its 1873 patent (see pages 8–9) was due to expire in 1890, Levi Strauss & Co. needed a simple and effective way of reminding consumers why its product was so great before a flurry of companies were able to jump on the blue-jean bandwagon. It proved a smart move.

The Two Horse logo remains one of the best examples of effective branding. Levi Strauss & Co. needed to give a message about the strength and functionality of its products in a way that could be instantly understood by anyone. The result was what we still see today: two horses trying in vain to tear a pair of Levi's in half. The genius of this logo is the understanding it shows of its market: not all of the Levi's consumer base could read English, and a decent percentage most likely couldn't read at all, so it was important that this logo gave the correct message without the use of language. With the creation of the Two Horse logo, Levi's had given everyone a universal symbol by which to describe its product – 'the pants with the two horses'. The product was even called 'The Two Horse Brand' up until 1928 when it adopted the Levi's trademark that we know today.

The Two Horse logo has been used by Levi Strauss & Co. continually since its creation in 1886, making it the fifth-oldest logo still in use to survive unchanged.

Opposite: The Two Horse logo is one of the world's most iconic, but few people know its history or origins today. Here we see the logo in the centre of a vintage advert, when it was presented more as a demonstration of product strength.

Levi's 'XX' with Two Horse logo

1886

In 1890 Levi Strauss & Co.'s patent expired and the company had to come up with ways to distinguish itself and its products from its competitors, who arrived on the market that year. With this in mind, Levi Strauss & Co. started printing the inside pocket bag with information on the strength and originality of the 'XX' denim waist coveralls, ensuring consumers knew who had got there first. Along with this change came the introduction of lot number 501, effectively rechristening the 'XX' with the product name that we have known the jean by ever since.

There seem to have been various reasons behind the name change, but it is largely attributed to the introduction of better stock management, enabling buyers to order by number rather than by description, as done in the past. Like its previous 'XX' name, '501' still referred to the standard of materials and manufacturing, with the '5' denoting the highest quality. The exact workings of the numbering system and reasons for the name changes in general are not known because Levi Strauss & Co. lost most of its records during the 1906 San Francisco earthquake when fire destroyed its factories and headquarters.

The '501' of 1890 was still made using the 9oz denim manufactured by the Amoskeag Manufacturing Company of Manchester, New Hampshire – the same denim used by Levi's since the creation of the blue jean in 1873 (see pages 8–9).

Opposite: These original Levi's '501' jeans dating from 1890 were found in an abandoned mine in Calico, California in 1948.

Levi's '501'

1890

Levi's '201'

Another much lesser-known product produced by Levi's in 1890 was the '201'. Using the same coding system as the '501' first issued that year (see pages 16–17), the lower number referred to the lower-quality materials and therefore lower price. A 'value' version of the now-famous '501' copper-riveted jean, the '201' was a smart pre-emptive move from Levi Strauss & Co., ensuring that, when its patent expired, it had a jean to compete with the products offered by undercutting competitors.

The '201' jean was still manufactured using denim from the Amoskeag Manufacturing Company, though it was not its high-quality 'XX' denim. The '201' also introduced a linen patch, as opposed to the traditional leather patch of the '501', a detail that remains today on the cheaper offerings from Levi Strauss & Co.

Although the '201' was discontinued around the time of World War II (strange considering that the quality of Levi's jeans was famously reduced at this time to cut back on manufacturing costs and the use of metal), the idea behind the '201' as a cheaper alternative to the best-selling Levi's jean is one that still resonates within the brand today and has played a significant part in its continuing success.

Opposite and below: A modern reproduction of the '201' jean, one of several products Levi Strauss & Co were producing by 1890.

19

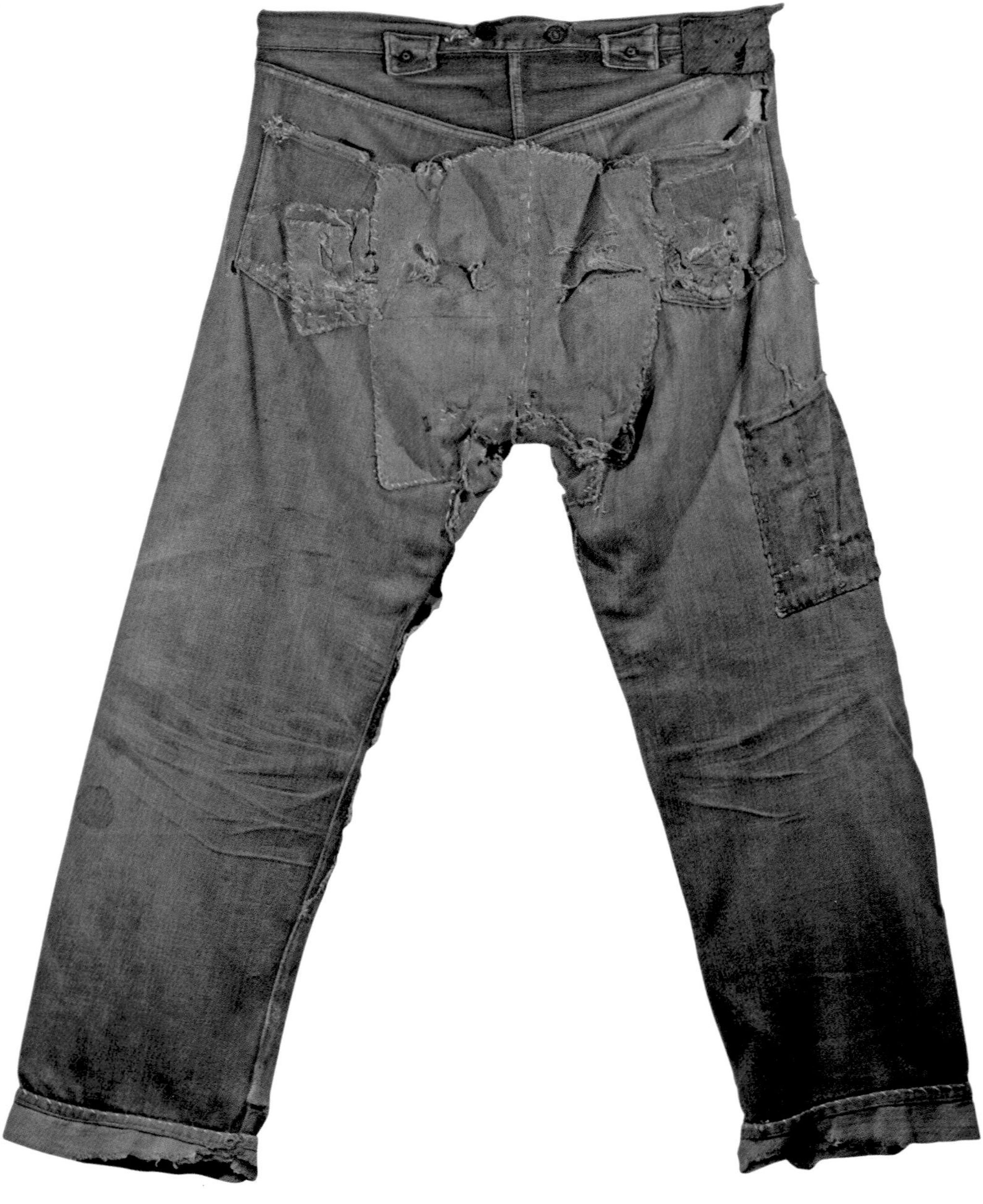

As the '501' developed over the years several additions and refinements were made. In 1901 Levi Strauss & Co. added the second back pocket, an addition that has remained ever since.

It's a bit strange to see a pair of jeans with only one back pocket today, but in 1901 it would have been the other way around. Even though this change was a large step towards the '501' we know today, there were still plenty of features from the originals still in use, such as the cinch and the suspender buttons (belt loops were yet to come). It's also worth noting that the back pockets on the 1901 '501' were widely spaced, pushing their way to the outer seams of the jeans, giving the jean a visual appeal that is admired by vintage '501' enthusiasts. This particular '501' has since been recreated by Levi's Vintage Clothing.

Although only a minor change, this refinement, along with the belt loops that joined the '501' in 1922 (pages 22–3), is now an essential and iconic part of a pair of jeans.

Opposite: These '501' jeans were bought in 1917 by Homer Campbell, an Arizona miner. He complained three years later that they hadn't lasted, although only the patches he had sewn on had worn through – the original jeans were intact.

Levi's '501' with second back pocket

1901

Levi's '501' with belt loops

Continuing the development of the '501' jean to reflect the cultural changes of the time, Levi Strauss & Co. added belt loops to the style in 1922.

Much like the addition of the second back pocket in 1901 (see pages 20–1), the addition of belt loops may seem rather minor, but it reflected a larger change in culture. A knock-on effect from the military uniforms of World War I, belts started featuring on civilian clothing not long after the conflict concluded. As time went on, the belt became increasingly important to the younger working man, and therefore to the Levi's customer and the denim market. Noticing this change in fashion and the functionality of clothing, Levi Strauss & Co. added belt loops to the '501'. However, conscious that its more traditional customer might not want to wear a belt, the suspender buttons and cinch were also left in place, allowing for the best of both worlds. Younger customers would cut off the cinch in order to make the jeans more comfortable when wearing a belt, a precursor to the removal of the cinch by the manufacturer in 1941 (see pages 36–7).

The year 1922 was also when Levi's gave exclusivity of its denim supplies to Cone Mills, a textile manufacturer based in Greensboro, North Carolina, which would become one of the most famous and revered denim manufacturers in the world. The 1922 '501' has since been recreated by Levi's Vintage Clothing.

Opposite and below: In order to move with the times, Levi Strauss & Co. added belt loops to the '501' jean in 1922. This pair from 1933 features both belt loops and a cinch, reflecting the split in the market.

Lee Cowboy Pants

LEE
Saddle Comfort
COWBOY PANTS

"Genuine Hair-On-Hide Label"

1. Sanforized-shrunk
2. 11½-oz. Denim
3. Copper Riveted Strain Points
4. Scratch Proof Hip Pockets
5. U-shaped Saddle Crotch

GUARANTEE: "If you do not find the Lee Cowboy Pants the best fitting and longest wearing you've ever worn, you can have a new pair free or your money back." *(Copr. 1938, The H. D. Lee Co.)*

THE H. D. LEE COMPANY
SAN FRANCISCO, CALIF.

JULY-AUGUST, 1941   THE WESTERN HORSEMAN   51

Lee
'Cowboy Pants'

1924

Having founded his company in 1889, Henry David Lee had quickly spotted promise in the workwear market, creating 8oz denim bib overalls in 1911. However, it wasn't until the mass success of his 'Union-All' work jumpsuit in 1913 that the Lee name gained major popularity in the United States.

In 1924 Lee created its first pair of jeans – the Lee 'Cowboy Pants'. Designed specifically to meet the needs of the cowboy and the rodeo rider, the 'Cowboy Pants' would prove one of the most important innovations for Lee. It not only signalled the company's move into the jeans market, but began its focus on cowboys and cowboy culture – the culture that would help to spread the jeanswear market throughout the world.

Given the stock number 101 (a number that would later go on to symbolize Lee's premium offerings with the Lee '101' line), the 'Cowboy Pants' proved hugely popular thanks to their tough 13oz denim. The 'Cowboy Pants' would later go on to be renamed the Lee 'Rider' in 1944. That year would also see the creation of the now-famous 'Lazy S' stitching on the back pockets, replacing the arcuate identical to the Levi's one that was used from 1924 to 1944, much like that found on most denim brands at this time.

With the creation of the 'Cowboy Pants', Lee had entered the jeans market and was there to stay. This significant moment also marks the beginning of the end for Lee's business in the workwear market.

Opposite: A 1941 advert for Lee's 'Saddle Comfort Cowboy Pants'. The back pockets of the jeans have the same arcuate stitching as Levi's jeans. This stitching was changed in 1944. Below: A pair of jeans from the Lee archive.

It's hard to believe now, but up until 1926 no one had thought of putting a zip-fly into jeans. It was strictly buttons only. This becomes even more surprising when you discover that the zip fastener had debuted in 1893, at the Chicago World's Fair, 33 years before Henry David Lee decided to put it into use in his 'Cowboy Pants'. That's a long time for someone to come up with an idea, but the world moved more slowly back then.

Denim workwear and jeanswear was still a very innovative market at this time and in 1926 Lee pushed the boundaries further, creating the world's first zip-fly jean, the '101Z'. The '101Z' was simply the Lee 'Cowboy Pants' (aka the '101'; see pages 24–5) with a zip-fly rather than a button-fly. With this creation, the 'Cowboy Pants' became known as either the '101B' or '101Z', depending on whether the fly was button- or zip-fastened. The year 1926 also saw the introduction of the popular U-shaped saddle crotch to the 'Cowboy Pants', as well as tailored sizing.

While Henry David Lee probably knew that this innovation would have a massive impact on workwear and cowboy attire, mainly thanks to its functionality, he surely had no idea of its future impact on fashion and style.

Opposite: Now taken for granted by many, the addition of a zip-fly to jeans was a major innovation in 1926.

27

Lee '101Z'

1926

No. 701

Although not the first female-specific products issued by Levi Strauss & Co., 'Lady Levi's' jeans for women were undoubtedly the company's first major success in the field.

Levi's first product designed specifically for women was the 'Freedom-Alls', launched in 1918. Resembling a belted tunic paired with harem pants, the 'Freedom-Alls' were a unique-looking product that didn't get the best reception, leading to their removal from catalogues and price lists the following year.

Fast-forward to 1934 and Levi's was ready to launch a new venture in the women's clothing market. 'Lady Levi's' mark a historical moment for Levi's, denim and fashion as a whole, being the first ever denim jeans designed for women. Manufactured from pre-shrunk denim, the jeans featured a high, nipped-in waist that gave them a fashionably feminine aesthetic. Other than fit and material, the 'Lady Levi's' shared many of the construction methods and materials of the masculine '501' jeans.

Considering the mass popularity of women's jeans, and more specifically fitted jeans, that would develop over the following decades, the 'Lady Levi's' marked a hugely important moment for style and fashion as the denim market continued to expand.

Opposite: 29
This original sketch of 'Lady Levi's' includes their '701' lot number, used to distinguish them from the popular '501' for men.

'Lady Levi's'

1934

'Lady Levi's' were 31
aimed at women
working on
ranches across
America. This
photograph is
from the 1930s.

Alongside the world-famous Two Horse logo (see pages 14–15), Levi's is well known for the arcuate design on the back pockets of its jeans. Hard to believe today, but when the Levi's patent expired in 1890 and competitors such as Stronghold, Boss of the Road and Can't Bust 'Em starting manufacturing riveted denim jeans, the pocket stitching on competitors' jeans looked very similar to that of Levi's. Frustrated by the similarity, the national sales manager, Chris Lucier, suggested that Levi's place 'a folded cloth ribbon in the structural seam of a rear patch pocket'. The idea was a good one, and Levi's started doing exactly that, stitching a red tab with 'LEVI'S' woven in white on to the right back pocket of every pair of '501' jeans. With the rich-red colour popping against the dark-blue indigo of the denim, it was now easy to distinguish a pair of Levi's from a distance and the red tab, or 'Tab Device' as it's officially called, was born.

Today the Tab Device is one of the most iconic parts of a pair of Levi's jeans and one of the most iconic features in the denim world as a whole. Levi Strauss & Co. knew how important this addition would be and throughout the 1940s and 1950s drew people's attention to it in marketing materials, which often featured the slogan 'Look for the Red Tab'.

Opposite: This 1937 pair of Levi's features an early example of the red tab. In 1971 Levi's changed the logo on the Tab Device from 'LEVI'S' to 'Levi's', and collectors have used the 'Big E' tab as a way of dating vintage denim ever since.

Levi's '501' with red tab

1936

Lee bootcut jean

1941

Following the success of its 'Cowboy Pants' (see pages 24–5) and the popularity of cowboy culture worldwide, Lee began to bring renowned cowboys on board as consultants. In 1941 Lee reached out to Thurkel ('Turk') Greenough, a rodeo star from a family of rodeo performers in Montana, asking him to help the company improve on its classic '101'.

Turk Greenough, along with his wife, burlesque dancer Sally Rand, re-tailored a pair of Lee 'Cowboy Pants', making them slightly tighter in general, but also giving the leg a slight flare to make room for Turk's riding boots. With these tweaks came the invention of what is now known as the bootcut jean. With the help of an expert in the field, Lee had once again innovated within the denim market, creating what would become a hugely popular fit among the cowboy community.

Later on, the bootcut jean would become one of the best-loved (but also most hated) denim styles in fashion, enjoying a second wind of popularity in the 1990s. Although less popular today, the bootcut is still available from most denim manufacturers.

Opposite: Sally Rand tailors rodeo star Turk Greenough's Lee jeans, creating the bootcut fit in 1941.
Below: An early example of the Lee bootcut jean.

In 1941 the United States entered World War II and the War Production Board set up by the US government declared that all clothing manufacturers were to remove a stipulated amount of fabric, metal and thread from their production processes in order to conserve raw materials as part of the war effort.

With these new restrictions in place, Levi's omitted the rivets from the watch pocket and crotch, as well as removing the cinch and its rivets and the suspender buttons. It was not an easy time for Levi's, which also had to remove the 'decorative' arcuate stitching from the back pockets. Because this was one of the important identifiers of a pair of Levi's, the company decided to paint the arcuate on the rear pockets instead. The paint often wore off quite quickly, but Levi's thought it important that '501s' were at least leaving the factory with a visible arcuate on the back pockets. Jeans from this era with the paint still intact have since become a sought-after collector's item and can fetch thousands of dollars at auction.

Although World War II and its manufacturing restrictions had a negative effect on Levi's at the time, the conflict also helped to take the brand, and denim culture as a whole, global. With American GIs wearing their jeans overseas, the rest of the world fell in love with denim.

Opposite: This original pair of Levi's '501' jeans from 1944 includes all the sales material that came with each pair, such as the 'guarantee ticket' attached to the the back pocket.

Levi's '501' during World War II

1941

Wrangler '11MWZ'

The Wrangler brand we know today has a rather complicated history. The story begins back in 1919 when the Hudson brothers from Tennessee renamed their workwear company – based in Greensboro, North Carolina – the Blue Bell Overall Company. Big Ben Manufacturing purchased the Blue Bell Overall Company in 1926 but retained the company name. Lastly, in 1943, Blue Bell acquired Casey Jones Company along with its rarely used Wrangler brand name. As I said, it's a complicated history.

In 1947 Blue Bell released a pair of Wrangler jeans designed by celebrity tailor Bernard Lichtenstein (aka 'Rodeo Ben') – the '11MWZ'. Designed for use by rodeo riders, the '11MWZ' featured both felled out-seams and in-seams, a lack of rivets to prevent saddle scratching, rear pocket positioning for comfort on the saddle, a zip-fly and a strongly tacked crotch. To help promote the new Wrangler brand, the company had the '11MWZ' wear-tested and endorsed for its quality and durability by professional rodeo cowboys Jim Shoulders, Bill Linderman and Freckles Brown.

In 1952 the '11MWZ' would be renamed the '13MWZ' in reference to its 13oz denim. Much like other denim brands of the time, the original Wrangler's featured the same arcuate stitching on the back pockets as Levi's, but this was soon replaced by the Wrangler 'W' stitching that we see today. The '13MWZ' was also the first pair of jeans to feature Wrangler's innovative broken twill denim in 1964, which gave it a softer feel and stopped the jeans from twisting. This same broken twill denim fabric would be used later by the likes of Calvin Klein (pages 58–9) and Nudie Jeans Co. (pages 108–9).

Opposite: An original pair of Wrangler '11MWZ' jeans. This style was heavily marketed to cowboys and remained the brand's most iconic jean for decades.

By the mid-1950s the United States wasn't the only country where denim jeans were being manufactured. M. Cooper (Overalls) Ltd. was a British-based company founded in London in 1908, making workwear much like that produced by the US companies that had inspired it. The company went on to manufacture uniforms for the British military during both world wars.

It was during World War II that co-founder (and, by that point, sole company owner) Morris Cooper died in a car crash, leaving the company to his son, Harold. On returning from service in the Royal Air Force, Harold set out to reposition the company, one aspect of which was to rename the company using an Americanized version of his wife's maiden name, Leigh – hence Lee Cooper. The other major change was to move the company into the denim jeans fashion market, again inspired by what was happening in the States at this time. The Lee Cooper brand took off quickly in the UK, picked up by almost every British subculture.

In 1952 Lee Cooper caused a moral uproar by placing a zip-fly at the front of its women's jeans. Up until this point, it had been considered too masculine or vulgar for women's trousers of any sort to have a front-facing fastening (button or zip) – traditionally, women's trousers always had side or back fastening systems. It was a ground-breaking moment for denim and for women's fashion in general.

Opposite: Almost 20 years after the introduction of 'Lady Levi's', Lee Cooper caused outrage when they created woman's jeans with a zip-fly at the front. Decades later, the idea of jeans and sex appeal had become inseparable.

Lee Cooper women's zip-flies

1952

The reception committee for
the new kid on the block!

JAMES DEAN

The overnight sensation of 'East of Eden'

Warner Bros. put
all the force of
the screen
into a challenging
drama of today's
juvenile violence!

"REBEL WITHOUT A CAUSE"

IN **CINEMASCOPE**
AND **WARNERCOLOR**

...and they both come
from 'good' families!

ALSO STARRING
NATALIE WOOD WITH SAL MINEO · JIM BACKUS · ANN DORAN · COREY ALLEN · WILLIAM HOPPER · STEWART STERN   MUSIC BY LEONARD ROSENMAN   PRODUCED BY DAVID WEISBART · DIRECTED BY NICHOLAS RAY   A WARNER BROS. PICTURE

The 1950s was an era of transition for denim, as it moved from being a symbol of traditional national pride, rooted in hard work and cowboy culture, to a symbol of youthful rebellion. One of the most important figures in this transition was Hollywood actor James Dean.

In 1955 James Dean starred in *Rebel Without a Cause*, a film about the growing gap between American youth and the preceding conservative generation, with the focus firmly on teenage angst. Throughout the film James Dean's character, Jim Stark, is seen wearing Dean's favourite jeans, the Lee '101', coupled with a tight, white T-shirt. It's a look that has become almost as iconic as the man himself. Tragically, James Dean died in a car crash only a month before the release of the film and so did not live to witness the large impact that he would have on both denim and style.

Although not the earliest moment in the love affair between denim and Hollywood, this was definitely one of the most important early examples and remains an iconic moment in denim history. It also signalled the start of the long-term relationship between denim and biker culture.

Opposite: An original poster for *Rebel Without a Cause* depicts James Dean in a well-worn pair of Lee '101' jeans. Following pages: James Dean's on-screen attitude helped change the image of jeans forever.

Lee '101' jeans worn in *Rebel Without a Cause*

1955

As the denim-clad style of the restless youth of America continued to gain traction throughout the 1950s, James Dean once again helped to secure Lee's place at the forefront of denim culture when he appeared – alongside Elizabeth Taylor – in the 1956 film *Giant*, this time wearing the Lee '101Z' (see pages 26–7)

In this film Dean played a more conventional role than in *Rebel Without a Cause*: Jett Rink, the ranch hand who becomes an oil millionaire. The film, although released after Dean's death, would go on to earn the actor his second posthumous nomination for Best Actor at the 1956 Academy Awards. Throughout the film Dean is seen sporting his Lee '101Z' jeans, often with his shirt unbuttoned down to his abdomen in a look that has become attached to the icon himself.

The value of James Dean's love for the Lee '101' jean proved immeasurable to Lee and the company would go on to use imagery of Dean in its marketing materials and PR for decades to follow. Lee Japan would later go on to reproduce the '101Z' jeans that Dean favoured, with painstaking attention to detail – as the Lee Japan '101Z 1952'.

Opposite: James Dean's life was cut tragicallly short, but his influence extended far beyond it, especially when it came to his love for Lee's '101' and '101Z' jeans.

47

Lee '101Z' worn in *Giant*

1956

Right at the peak of his career, Elvis Presley starred in the movie *Jailhouse Rock*. Featured in the movie was an experiment from the Levi's brand – black denim. Originally named (somewhat uncreatively) the Levi's 'Elvis Presley' jeans, they were aimed at the new 'rebellious youth' market, and Levi's had savvily attached itself to the subculture's leader, Elvis Presley.

Ironically, Elvis Presley actually disliked jeans, associating them with the hard work and poverty that he had spent his life trying to escape. It was exactly this image that Levi's (and denim as a whole) needed to shake off. Up until 1956 Levi's had focused its branding and marketing on glorifying the Gold Rush era, but this wasn't connecting with the youth of the 1950s. This was where the black 'Elvis Presley' jeans came into play.

This moment holds huge significance in fashion and culture for a couple of reasons. Firstly, it's the birth of the black jean, an item of clothing that has since gone on to become a style icon in its own right. Secondly, their association with Elvis Presley and their endorsement in *Jailhouse Rock* made a significant contribution to jeans becoming a must-have item for the youth of the 1950s, helping Levi's to compete against its major rival, Lee, which was making heavy use of film appearances at the time (see pages 42–7).

Opposite: Although not a fan of jeans himself, Elvis made a huge impact on the world of denim when he agreed to work with Levi's to create the first black jeans in 1956.

Levi's 'Elvis Presley' jeans

1956

Edwin '359BF'

1963

The Edwin brand was created by the Japanese clothing entrepreneur Shuji Tsunemi in 1961 and has played a hugely important role in Japan's denim history.

After studying in the United States, Shuji Tsunemi returned to Japan, where he inherited the family business, a U.S. military surplus store established in Tokyo in 1947. In 1961, realizing the potential of denim, Tsunemi founded his own brand – Edwin – a name that derives from the letters found in the word 'denim', if the 'm' is turned upside down to form a 'w'. He started importing denim from America and produced his first pair of jeans that year. These are said to be the first jeans manufactured in Japan, although other companies, including Maruo Clothing (see pages 52–3), also claim to have been there first.

In 1963 Edwin launched the '359BF', made from 16oz Peruvian denim, the heaviest ringspun denim in the world at the time. These jeans featured the three-colour rainbow selvage that Edwin still uses today. Edwin has continued to innovate in the world of denim and is still one of the most successful denim brands to come from Japan.

The creation of the Edwin brand marks an important moment in the denim story: the time when Japan entered into denim manufacturing. Today, Japanese denim is regarded as some of the best-quality denim in the world.

Opposite and below: One of the first denim brands from Japan, Edwin has gone on to become one of the best-known denim brands in the world.

The Tsunemi KK company (see pages 50–1) wasn't the only one importing used American jeans into the Japanese market in the wake of World War II. Maruo Clothing had also spotted the market for imported denim from the States, laundered and resized for the Japanese consumer. Thanks to Japan's new obsession with US culture, it was a booming industry.

In April 1965 Maruo Clothing, in partnership with Canton Textile Mills and Oishi Trading Company, manufactured a pair of jeans at the Kurabo Mill in Kojima, Japan, under the Canton brand name. The jeans were manufactured on the now-famous Toyoda machines from 50 rolls of denim imported from the Canton Textile Mills in Canton, Georgia (hence the name). Accustomed to pre-worn denim, the Japanese consumers didn't favour the raw variety, and in October 1965 Maruo Clothing produced the world's first one-wash jeans. This moment is often credited as the start of the washed-denim craze.

After the success of its Canton jeans, Maruo Clothing started working on a prototype for a new brand of its own using denim from Cone Mills. It would be called Big John (pages 54–5) and would become one of the most important Japanese denim brands.

Canton by Maruo Clothing

1965

Big John 'M' series

Not long after releasing its first Japanese manufactured pair of jeans under the Canton brand (pages 52–3), Maruo Clothing began working on its own jeans brand, Big John.

The first jeans for the Big John brand were called 'M1002' and were manufactured using denim imported from Cone Mills in the United States, the same mills that Levi's had been using exclusively since 1922. Launched in 1968 as the first 'M' series, the line included the 'M1002' (straight fit), 'M2002' (bootcut) and 'M3002' (slim fit) and were all sewn in Japan. The original prototype for the 'M1002' in 1967 was actually sewn in the United States, but the products that were released to market were constructed in Japan.

Not content with simply manufacturing the jeans in Japan, Maruo Clothing worked alongside the Kurabo Mill to create Japan's first ever domestic denim in 1972. It took eight attempts, but finally Japan had its own denim in the form of KD-8 fabric (short for 'Kurabo Denim 8'). The following year Big John released the 'M' series, manufactured in Japan using KD-8 denim fabric.

In one of the most momentous denim moments to happen outside of the United States, Japan finally had a pair of jeans that it could rightfully claim were 100 per cent Japanese. This was the beginning of Japanese manufactured denim.

Opposite: The birth of the Japanese denim industry has had a huge effect on the design and production of denim and jeans around the world.

In 1977 Calvin Klein changed the world of denim by introducing Calvin Klein Jeans to the market, allegedly selling 200,000 pairs in the first week.

It started in 1976 when Klein included slim-fitting jeans in his catwalk collection – the first time that jeans had been featured in a fashion show. However, it wasn't until he made a few tweaks to the design the following year, accentuating the crotch and buttocks, that Calvin Klein Jeans was born and became an instant success.

On their release to the public, Calvin Klein jeans were the must-have item in fashion, elevating jeans in the eyes of the fashion consumer. With one simple move, Calvin Klein had created the designer denim market that would continue to boom for the next ten years and that still continues to produce new products and brands to this day. Decades later, designer denim would create everything from the artisan Evisu jeans (pages 80–1), to the trendy Dior Homme jeans (pages 104–5) and, more recently, the Junya Watanabe patchwork jeans (page 120–1).

This Calvin Klein subbrand would not only revolutionize denim as a consumer product, but also how it was advertised and perceived, breaking ground and changing denim for ever.

Opposite: Calvin Klein included slim-fitting denim in a 1976 fashion show – the first time jeans appeared on the catwalk.

Calvin Klein Jeans

1977

A few years after Calvin Klein Jeans (see pages 58–9) kicked off the designer denim craze, the brand would create one of the most controversial advertising campaigns fashion had ever seen.

Photographed and directed by Richard Avedon and featuring the 15-year-old actress Brooke Shields, the campaign used the now-famous line 'Do you want to know what comes between me and my Calvins? Nothing.' The advertising campaign was striking, evocative and controversial – adjectives that could be applied to a lot of Calvin Klein's adverts in the decades that followed. After multiple complaints the advert was banned by many TV networks, but by that time it had already had the desired effect, pushing sales of Calvin Klein Jeans to 2 million pairs a month.

The use of sex to sell jeans has been around almost as long as jeans themselves: early-1960s Lee campaigns had used images of women pointing at a man in Lee jeans with the tagline 'There's my man! … In those smart-looking Lee Cowboy Pants!' – though in those days things were a lot more subtle and allusive. In 1980 Calvin Klein Jeans stepped it up several gears and associated tight-fitting jeans with sexiness forever.

The company's sexy, savvy advertising campaigns would go on to launch the careers of several famous models, including Kate Moss and Mark Wahlberg (see pages 84–5).

Brooke Shields in Calvin Klein Jeans

1980

Big John 'RARE'

1980

Already a name for its innovative approach to denim – largely thanks to its 'M' series in 1973 (pages 54–5) – Big John created another game-changing pair of jeans in 1980: its RARE jeans with lot number R001.

The most significant innovation in the development of 'RARE' jeans was the creation of the world's first purposely uneven yarns – that is, yarns with areas of increased thickness along the thread. This creates denim with a more unique character, especially with regard to how it develops with age. The 'RARE' jeans were manufactured on power shuttle looms, creating Japan's first ever selvage denim, among various other obsessive details of quality. 'RARE' jeans were, and still are, about the best of the best, using the best craftsmen in Japan for every part of the process.

Japanese selvage denim would go on to become some of the most highly regarded in the world. The 'RARE' jeans by Big John are often credited for inspiring the rise of vintage and replica jeans, and future Japanese brands such as Evisu (pages 80–1) as well as the rise of premium denim in the mid-1990s.
In 1997 Big John would take the 'RARE' concept a step further with their 'RARE Meister' jeans (pages 98–9).

Opposite: Big John 'RARE' jeans mark the beginning of Japanese selvage denim, one of the most highly regarded denims in the world today.

Having fled from France, allegedly to avoid a hefty tax bill, the Moroccan-born brothers Georges and Maurice Marciano opened their own fashion store in Beverly Hills in 1981. The store sold jeans designed by Georges Marciano under the GUESS Inc. brand name and featuring the now-iconic triangle logo on the back.

That same year Georges Marciano flew to New York City with his jeans, convincing Bloomingdale's to stock 30 pairs and display them in its flagship store. It proved a wise move, with all 30 pairs selling out in under three hours. GUESS Inc.'s stone-washed jeans with their European slim fit and zippered ankles were an instant success.

Not only was GUESS Inc. an important player in the success of stone-washed denim, it also changed how denim brands were advertised. By 1982 Paul Marciano had joined the company and began to direct its advertising, taking the jeans and the models wearing them out of the studio – the setting that until then had been commonplace for designer denim shoots – and on to the streets. Shooting on grainy black-and-white film, the advertising campaigns were provocative and sexy, turning many of the previously unknown models, or 'GUESS Girls', into household names – along with the GUESS Inc. brand itself.

Opposite: Unlike the original triangle logo shown here, today the company's logo reads 'GUESS® U.S.A.' However, it still features the phrase 'WASHED JEANS', proudly declaring what first made the brand famous.

GUESS Inc.

1981

In 1984 Bruce Springsteen's career exploded thanks to his album *Born in the USA.* At the time, Springsteen symbolized all things American and his 1984 release pushed that to its limits: on the cover of the LP, against the backdrop of an American flag, was a close-up of the singer's rear in a worn-in pair of Levi's '501' jeans.

Born in the USA would go on to be the US bestselling album of 1985, as well as Springsteen's most successful album of all time. A slight change in musical direction, teamed with an overhaul of his image, had helped push both Springsteen and *Born in the USA* to a much wider audience than his previous records. With this huge popularity, a strong focus on Americana and '501' jeans on the cover, it's no surprise that every cool kid wanted a pair following the release of this album. Shot by Annie Leibovitz, the album cover would propel Springsteen to pop icon status, breathing new life into the '501' at the same time.

Since the album's release, the cover for *Born in the USA* has gone on to become one of the most iconic of all time, as well as one of the most iconic moments of denim in popular culture.

Opposite: The Levi's '501' jeans worn by Bruce Springsteen take pride of place on the cover of *Born in the USA.* One of the most iconic album covers of all time, it continues to create interest in the Levi's brand today.

67

Levi's '501' on the cover of *Born in the USA*

1984

Having only launched four years prior, GUESS Inc. (see pages 64–5) achieved its best product placement ever in 1985, by creating all of the denim clothing for Michael J. Fox's character Marty McFly in *Back to the Future*.

Marty McFly's stone-washed denim jeans and jacket make up part of one of Hollywood's most iconic character outfits, and they were custom made for the film by GUESS Inc. Although the company was already a huge success by 1985, getting its product on to the lead character of the highest-grossing film of the year undoubtedly had its benefits and the company continued to reap the rewards for decades after.

Back to the Future and its two sequels, released in 1989 and 1990, would go on to become one of the most successful film series of all time. Although GUESS Inc. only provided Marty McFly's clothes for the first film, that denim outfit still remains a particularly memorable design choice from a series that includes some of Hollywood's most beloved outfits, props and examples of product placement, such as Marty's hoverboard or his Nike Air Mag self-lacing sneakers, both of which first appear in *Back to the Future II*.

Opposite: 69

Dressed in custom made denim by GUESS Inc., Marty McFly (Michael J. Fox, shown here with Claudia Wells) symbolized 1980s cool in *Back to the Future*.

GUESS Inc. jeans worn in *Back to the Future*

1985

Rifle Jeans
acid-wash denim

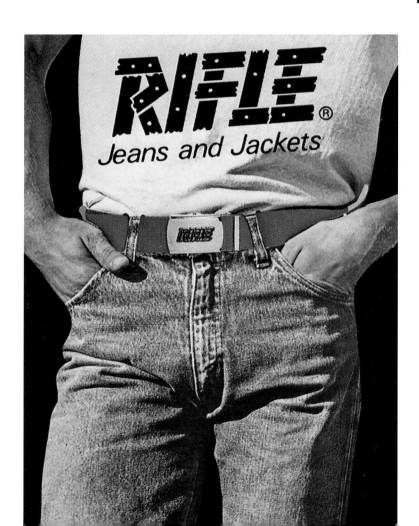

Acid wash is one of the most key visual developments in the history of denim, and helped to create one of the more iconic looks of the 1980s.

The technique was first brought to market by Italian brand Rifle Jeans in 1985, rapidly booming into a style craze around the world. Soon after its creation, acid-wash denim would become one of the most important parts of 1980s style. Don't let the name mislead you – the technique doesn't actually use acid, but chlorine, which gives a unique character to the denim. Pumice stones are impregnated with a chemical bleaching agent and put into the drying drum along with the denim, bleaching and scratching the denim at the same time.

Acid-wash jeans ushered in an era of heavily faded denim, which took the popular washed-denim look and pushed it further. By the late 1980s the light-denim trend was firmly established and would run on into the mid-1990s. Some American retailers in the late 1980s even went so far as to claim that the invention of acid-wash denim was the most important thing to happen to men's and women's clothing in years.

Although not as popular today as it was in the past, there's still plenty of acid-wash denim in various forms on the shelves of fashion retailers.

Opposite: With acid-wash denim, Rifle Jeans inadvertently created a trend for light jeans that would take the world by storm.

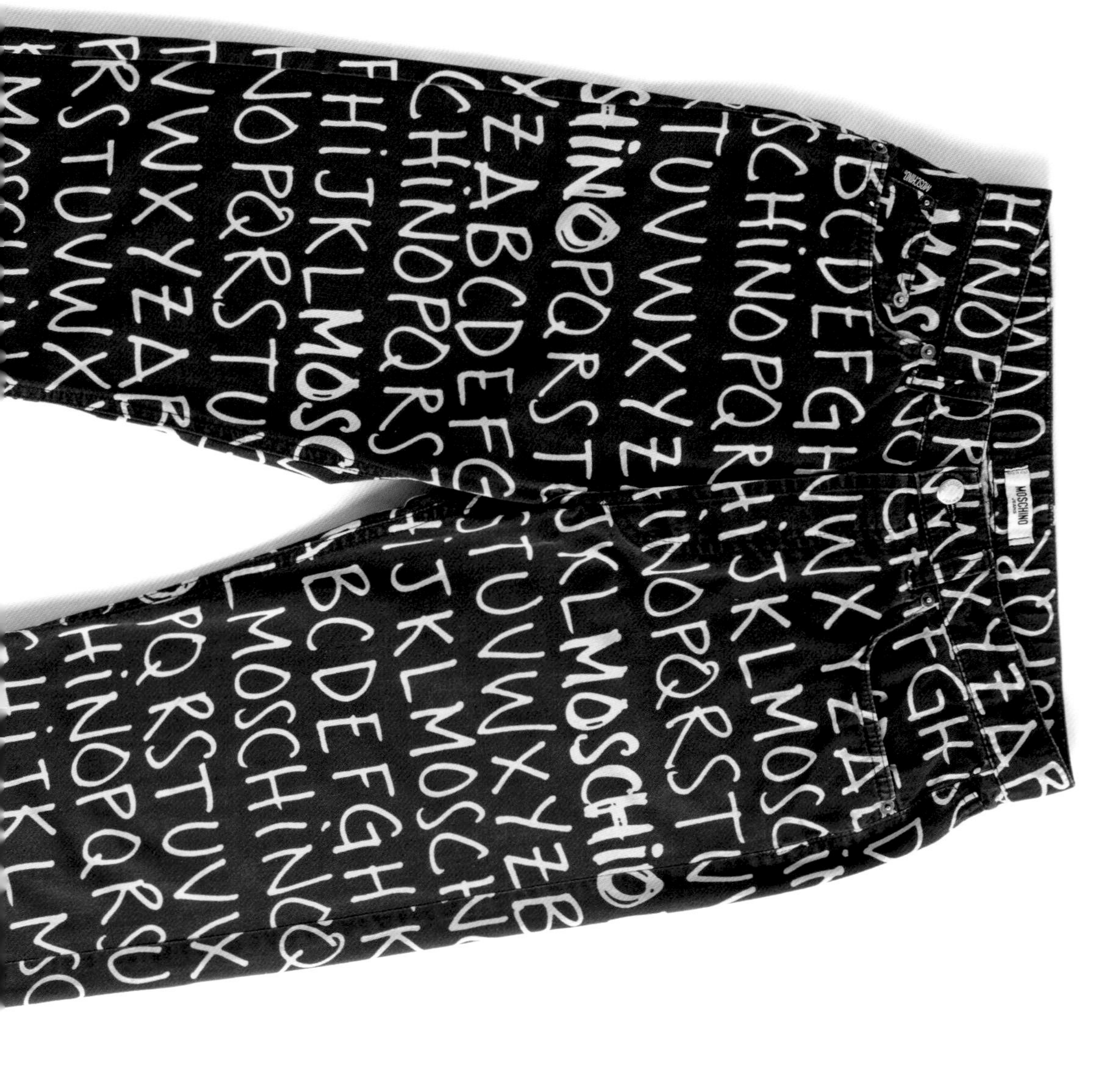

In 1983 Franco Moschino left his position as illustrator at Gianni Versace and launched his own label, which embodied his outsider viewpoint on the high-fashion industry and turned heads in doing so. His collections and shows were out of the ordinary and quickly earned him a reputation for being fearless, bold and eccentric.

In 1986 the maverick designer launched Moschino Jeans, a denim-inspired diffusion line that put the daring spirit of the main Moschino line into more ready-to-wear silhouettes and fabrics. The Moschino Jeans line was less exclusive than its high-fashion counterpart, enabling the brand to reach out to a much wider audience. Its bold use of colour and pattern struck a chord with the burgeoning rave culture in the UK in the late 1980s, so that Moschino became a staple part of the uniform for almost all UK underground dance music cultures throughout the 1990s. Today it's best known for its ties to the UK 1990s garage scene, still instantly recognizable in photographs and videos from the time, and there is a healthy second-hand and vintage market of collectors and enthusiasts.

In 2008 the Moschino Jeans line was renamed Love Moschino in an attempt to attract interest back to the brand.

Opposite: Print-laden Moschino jeans such as these were hugely popular in the UK garage scene, becoming a distinctive element of the culture itself.

Moschino Jeans

1986

A.P.C. (short for Atelier de Production et de Création) was founded in 1987 by Parisian designer Jean Touitou as a reaction to the bold, brash fashion of the 1980s. Since its inception, A.P.C. has become well known for its passion for minimalism and lack of branding.

From the very beginning, denim was a staple part of the A.P.C. business. The story goes that Touitou was inspired by the raw denim from army surplus stores that he used to wear in the 1960s, so he approached a denim specialist in Japan to help him replicate the material. A.P.C. offers its jeans in four fits, again playing to the rules of minimalism and perfectionism that the brand was founded upon. The 'New Standard' has become something of a cult jean in the world of denim. Its sleek, minimal design and slim fit without being overly tight have made it a menswear wardrobe essential. It's the jean's versatility, sleekness and high-quality Japanese raw denim that have enabled it to remain one of the most popular modern classics.

Considering that A.P.C. and the 'New Standard' were created at a time when acid wash (see pages 70–1) was all the rage, Touitou's super-clean, raw-denim jeans were a bold move, with a fittingly bold name. Supposedly, the cut of the A.P.C. 'New Standard' was the inspiration for Hedi Slimane's jeans at Dior Homme (pages 104–5).

Opposite: At a time when extreme washes and loud prints were all the rage, Jean Touitou started a quiet revolution with his brand A.P.C. and its minimal 'New Standard' jean.

A.P.C. 'New Standard'

1987

76 Opposite and below: Minimal branding, slim fit and high-quality denim have made the A.P.C. 'New Standard' jean a wardrobe essential.

Diesel's 'For Successful Living' ad campaign

As much as Calvin Klein and other fashion houses had built the image of jeans into an international symbol for sex appeal and style, Diesel were about to use that reputation and flip it on its head for their debut advertising campaign in 1991.

It may be hard to believe but Diesel hadn't done a campaign before 1991. In fact, the brand hadn't even had a consistent logo since its inception in 1978. The 1990s changed all that, mainly thanks to Diesel's newly appointed advertising director, Maurizio Marchiori. Working alongside Swedish agency Paradiset, Marchiori created an advertising campaign that took the notion of 'products making better living' from classic 1950s advertising and blew it out of proportion in a series of ironic adverts under the 'For Successful Living' tagline.

The adverts took an extremely exaggerated, often mocking view of fashion, advertising, denim culture and anything else that was loosely relevant. The campaigns went so far that a lot of people simply didn't get them. You either understood what Diesel were about, or you didn't, and it was this exclusivity in its communication that garnered the brand a lot of attention from affluent teenagers who were seeking ways to separate themselves from the norm.

Although the brand had been around for over 20 years by this point, it was the 'For Successful Living' campaigns of the 1990s that established the Diesel we know today. The brand was firmly on the map and the branded strip on the jean coin pocket would become an instantly recognizable motif.

Opposite: Launched in 1991, Diesel's provocative 'For Successful Living' campaign became a long-running, award-winning success story for the company.

In 1991 a young Japanese designer from Osaka, Hidehiko Yamane, launched his premium denim brand, Evisu.

Named after the Japanese god of money and fishing, Ebisu, the brand was founded on the principles of high-quality denim-wear manufactured using traditional, labour-intensive methods. Indeed, production was initially so time-consuming that Yamane could produce only 14 pairs per day, signing each pair with a hand-painted seagull on each back pocket.

To speed things up, or so the story goes, Yamane purchased an old American loom previously used to make Levi's. More recently, though, the Kurabo Mill that first produced Evisu jeans has confirmed that its shuttle looms at the time were in fact made by Japan's Toyoda (later renamed Toyota).

Whatever the origin of the loom, it was traditional manufacturing methods that Evisu used to create small numbers of premium denim jeans. Evisu is often credited for the global rise of premium denim, being the first brand to be able to sell jeans for over $100 (and get away with it) and one of the earliest Japanese denim brands to enjoy global success and recognition. Throughout the 1990s Evisu found loyal fans in the streetwear and hip-hop communities, and was eventually invited to show at London Fashion Week in 2000.

Loved by some, hated by others, the Evisu seagull is one of the most widely recognized logos in denim.

Opposite: Evisu has played with the instantly recognizable seagull motif on its jeans in numerous ways over the decades.

Evisu

1991

VERSACE
JEANS COUTURE

LONDON: 92 BROMPTON ROAD • 34/38 OLD BOND STREET - GLASGOW: THE ITALIAN CENTRE

During a period of rapid expansion through diversification in the early 1990s, Gianni Versace launched yet another sub-brand called Versace Jeans Couture in 1991 and entered the designer denim market.

Versace Jeans Couture was the Versace casual line, with a focus on jeans and all-over print shirts, much like the Moschino Jeans line (see pages 72–3). Also like Moschino, the Versace Jeans Couture brand would find a devoted audience in the underground dance music subcultures of Britain – again thanks to the use of bright colours, bold prints and expensive price tags. The UK garage scene and its love for opulence just couldn't resist the iconic branding and high price point (some jeans retailed for $200). In clubs, the black leather patch on the back of jeans with the gold metal emblem became a symbol both of style and wealth.

At a time when the market for denim was exploding and jeans covered in loud prints were the must-have item, it made complete sense for Versace to expand into this category. And they did very well from it. Along with the likes of Moschino and Iceberg History, Versace jeans remain emblematic of 1990s and early-2000s fashion and club culture.

Opposite: The first Versace Jeans Couture adverts pitched the luxury denim brand in much the same style as the Calvin Klein Jeans campaign of the early 1980s – clean, minimal and sexy.

Versace Jeans Couture

1991

Calvin Klein ad campaign featuring Kate Moss and Marky Mark

1992

Not a brand known for shying away from controversy – in fact, quite the opposite (see pages 60–1) – Calvin Klein Jeans launched an advertising campaign in 1992 that would once again garner major attention, while simultaneously launching the career of the young Kate Moss.

The campaign featured rapper Marky Mark (now better known as actor Mark Wahlberg) and the relatively unknown Kate Moss, both half naked, wearing only Calvin Klein underwear and Calvin Klein jeans. In the TV advert Marky Mark says: 'The best protection against AIDS is to keep your Calvins on' – a provocative statement for an advert that was launched at the peak of the AIDS crisis. Once again, Calvin Klein had created an advertising campaign that gained his brand huge attention – both positive and negative.

This advert and the casting of Marky Mark made a deliberate association between the brand and hip-hop – a relationship that many designer denim brands, notably Tommy Hilfiger (page 100–01), would build on throughout the 1990s.

This remains one of the most famous campaigns Kate Moss has been involved in, as well as one of the most controversial Calvin Klein campaigns ever made. It also created some of the most memorable images of designer denim.

Opposite: Calvin Klein's 1992 campaign featured Kate Moss and Marky Mark, seen here backstage at the photo shoot. Below: Moss would go on to star in a number of memorable campaigns for Calvin Klein during the 1990s – this billboard is from 1999.

The 1990s saw denim culture and hip-hop come together. Calvin Klein would work with Marky Mark (pages 84–5), while Tommy Hilfiger would team up with Aaliyah (pages 100–01). Hip-hop was becoming a global force and brands were trying to work out how to align themselves with it for maximum effect.

At this time, a small brand would start in Queens, New York, and become a global giant in its own right. That brand, called FUBU, was founded in 1992 by Daymond John. The FUBU brand gained rapid attention through skilful product placement and endorsements, as it worked tirelessly to ensure its products were worn by the biggest hip-hop stars in the best music videos throughout the 1990s. FUBU grew quickly, becoming one of the fastest-growing fashion brands in American history.

One of the stars who helped fuel this popularity was LL Cool J, who was often seen wearing FUBU and even managed to wear a FUBU hat in a Gap TV commercial (the advert was soon pulled by Gap once it realized). Throughout the 1990s FUBU grew to become a global giant, grossing $350 million dollars at its peak in 1998.

FUBU's success marks the moment when hip-hop culture began creating its own brands, rather than reinterpreting others. FUBU inspired, and did the groundwork for, the countless hip-hop-related brands to come.

Opposite: FUBU represents the start of brands coming from the hip-hop world, rather than being created for it.

87

FUBU

1992

As denim and hip-hop continued their love affair, rap legend Tupac Shakur would start a style trend that would forever be attached to the genre and the era – denim overalls.

Denim overalls had solid roots in workwear and US working-class culture, and you could style them pretty much however you wanted (as people would go on to do). Tupac was the king of this style, always wearing a pair of crisp Dickies overalls. Later on he'd get them customized by having 'THUG LIFE' embroidered across the stomach of the overalls to mimic his famous tattoo.

The denim overall found huge success in the 1990s as everyone from Tupac to Aaliyah to Rachel from *Friends* sported the look. Several people, usually in the music world, have attempted to bring back the look since, with varied success. In recent years the denim overall has enjoyed a comeback in the form of shorts, but the overalls still haven't managed to return as a men's style piece, as much as Justin Bieber has tried (badly) to make it happen. No one will do it as well as Tupac did. The only person who got close was Eminem in the early 2000s, wearing the exact same pair of Dickies overalls.

Opposite: A big fan of Dickies denim overalls in the early 1990s, Tupac had a customized pair with 'THUG LIFE' embroidered across the front – a reference to his famous tattoo.

Dickies overalls worn by Tupac

1993

This denim brand started life as Gap Star in 1989, becoming G-Star shortly after in order to distance itself from a company with a similar name. It wasn't until 1996 that it became the G-Star RAW brand we are familiar with today.

Designer Pierre Morisset took the young Dutch brand in a new direction when he focused it on 'raw' denim, creating a world-famous brand and unlocking a wealth of opportunity. A gritty, urban look and style quickly became synonymous with G-Star RAW, led by the brand's raw, unwashed denim and helped by some of its soon-to-become iconic cuts such as the 'Elwood' jean with its biker styling. G-Star RAW was soon known as a specialist in raw denim, as well as gaining a reputation for experimentation in denim design, often inspired by military uniforms. To this day, the brand has struggled to shift its image as a raw denim specialist, while the impact of its success and experimentation in this area has created a legacy of brands in its wake, such as fellow Dutch denim brand Denham.

G-Star RAW has become one of the largest denim brands in the world. Still viewed by many as an urban, casual brand, G-Star RAW has in recent years attempted to move its image further into the high end of the fashion market in an attempt to expand its customer base and influence, often acting more like a fashion house than a traditional denim brand.

Opposite: G-Star RAW has enjoyed huge global success ever since the brand first introduced its raw unwashed denim in 1996.

G-Star RAW

1996

The replication of vintage jeans is a movement that can be credited to consumers rather than brands. Originally spawned by the Japanese obsession for vintage Levi's, long before the brand noticed the market's potential, this lust for reproductions of old denim in East Asia led to Levi's introducing replicas to the Japanese market around 1987.

After the success of these replicas, Levi's created the 'Capital E' line for the American market in 1992, signified by the use of the block-capital branding on the Tab Device introduced in 1936 (see pages 32–3). In 1971 Levi's had changed its Tab Device to read 'Levi's' rather than 'LEVI'S'. However, the only letter to change visibly was the 'e', hence the name 'Capital E'. The line was created as a premium denim line using only single-stitch sewing machines, sewn by hand, in the same style as the original Levi's jeans.

Building on the popularity of its 'Capital E' line and the growing interest in denim heritage, Levi's created Levi's Vintage Clothing (LVC) in 1996. Based in Amsterdam under the Levi's XX division, the new brand would specialize in reproducing historical Levi's jeans and clothing from the Levi Strauss & Co. Archives in San Francisco, replicating them as closely as physically possible. Every aspect, from stitching to material to manufacturing process and even details such as swing tags, was re-created with meticulous precision by the LVC team.

LVC continues to produce two collections a year and its loyal fan base continues to grow. The creation of LVC helped Levi's put an increased focus on its brand history and continue to remind people of its past and heritage.

Opposite and below: The Levi's Vintage Clothing brand is all about heritage detail. This selection of Levi Strauss & Co. branding from across the decades shows the vast scale of the company's product range.

Levi's Vintage Clothing

1996

Thanks to Levi's
Vintage Clothing,
pieces from the
brand's archive
(opposite) are
brought back to
life in the form
of replicas.

95

The story of ACNE and the ACNE Action Jeans is an interesting one, and stands slightly outside of the norm in comparison to all the other brands featured in this book.

The brand started life as part of a multifaceted creative studio, based in Stockholm, Sweden, under the ACNE name (the acronym stands for Ambition to Create Novel Expressions). The ACNE collective focused on graphic design, production, film, advertising and video games. To embody what the ACNE collective was about, co-founder Jonny Johansson created 100 pairs of raw denim jeans with red stitching. Made by hand on a single-stitch machine, it is easy to spot one of the original 100 pairs today thanks to their imperfections. Johansson gave all 100 pairs away to friends and family as an experiment and soon gained the attention of major global publications such as *Wallpaper** and *Vogue*. Stores all over the world began asking to stock the jeans and the ACNE brand we know today was born. This time, though, the jeans were manufactured in Italy and they were quickly followed by full men's and women's lines.

Thanks to the unique way in which this brand was launched (almost by accident), ACNE Action Jeans has become a key case study in the development of contemporary marketing.

Opposite: From its unconventional beginnings in a Stockholm creative studio, ACNE Action Jeans has grown into a respected fashion brand.

ACNE
Action Jeans

1997

Ever keen to push the quality of denim manufacture, Big John took its 'RARE' concept from 1980 (see pages 62–3) even further with the creation of the 'RARE Meister' jeans in 1997.

Following the same guidelines of exceptional quality that the original 1980 'RARE' jeans were built on, the hand-made 'RARE Meister' jeans also introduced natural indigo dye. This brought the manufacturing process even closer to the original process that Levi's would have used for their 'XX' jeans (pages 8–9). The 'RARE Meister' jeans proved a huge success, with the entire limited run of 300 pairs selling out soon after they became available for pre-order.

Thanks to the pioneering 'RARE' jeans of 1980, as well as the premium denim brands that had been inspired by them, the world was more than ready for the latest super-premium offering from Big John. Although Big John released a third style of 'RARE' jeans in 2010 named 'NEW RARE R008', celebrating the 30th anniversary of Big John 'RARE', the 'RARE Meister' was the last range of truly innovative 'RARE' jeans.

Opposite: The attention to detail lavished on the Big John 'RARE Meister' jeans was carried through into their packaging and presentation.

Big John
'RARE Meister'

1997

Throughout the 1990s many fashion brands and designers were attaching themselves to the hip-hop phenomenon, but none were doing it quite like designer Tommy Hilfiger.

Hilfiger could see the importance of this culture and wanted his company to be seen to support it. Not only did he make sure that leading stars were seen wearing his Hilfiger Denim and Tommy Jeans brands, but he enlisted hip-hop's leading musicians to be the faces of his labels, including Usher, Snoop Dog and Aaliyah. Various hip-hop artists featured in Tommy Jeans commercials and catwalk shows, but it is Aaliyah who will forever be associated with the designer.

In 1997 Aaliyah shot a TV commercial for Tommy Jeans that featured the star dressed head to toe in the brand's iconic colours. Her style of baggy jeans, boxer shorts and tube top were a 1990s classic all on their own, but the commercial also signifies how fashion brands as a whole were starting to buy into hip-hop culture in a big way. Today the combination of Aaliyah and oversized, all-over Tommy Hilfiger branding has made this commercial an iconic moment for both 1990s style and nostalgia.

Opposite: Aaliyah is shown dressed head to toe in striking Tommy Jeans attire. The singer, who died in a plane crash aged 22 in 2001, and the label will forever be connected in pop-culture memory.

Tommy Jeans commercial featuring Aaliyah

1997

Walé Adeyemi
Graffiti Collection

As hip-hop culture continued to influence the world of fashion, more and more brands and young designers began to take it on in their work, and not only in the United States. In the UK the young Walé Adeyemi printed his graffiti-inspired writing on to denim jeans and jackets as part of his 1998 Graffiti Collection. The range would become hugely popular in the UK hip-hop and R&B community, quickly putting both Walé Adeyemi and his B-side brand on the global stage.

Following the success of his debut collection, Adeyemi went on to style and design for some of the world's brightest musical talents, including Alicia Keys and Estelle. His Graffiti Collection also gained him major recognition: in 2005 it was featured in the 'Moments in Black British Style' exhibition at London's Victoria and Albert Museum, and in 2008 Walé was awarded an MBE for his contributions to British fashion.

Walé's graffiti-inspired handwriting has gone on to become one of the most iconic typefaces of recent decades. It's hard to not see it replicated in some shape or form when walking through any of the major cities of the world. Unfortunately, today, it's better known for appearing on tourist merchandise than in its original form, on denim under Walé Adeyemi's B-side brand. Regardless, Adeyemi's name and the 1998 collection will forever remain an important part of British hip-hop and fashion history.

Opposite and below: Walé Adeyemi's Graffiti Collection features one of the most iconic typefaces of recent years.

After four years as head of Yves Saint Laurent Pour Homme, Hedi Slimane left to head Dior Homme, debuting his first collection for the brand in 2001. Although his collections at YSL were a prelude to what he would go on to do at Dior Homme, it was his work at the latter fashion house that saw him truly express his vision of the future of male fashion – the 'skinny' look that would forever become attached to his name.

It was a time where men's fashion was still feeling the after-effects of the 1990s jock-bodied model as the fashion industry's idea of the perfect male form (see, for example, the young Mark Wahlberg in the Calvin Klein advert on page 84). Slimane, however, had a different vision, one inspired by the indie boys of London and their skinny frames. Along with bringing pale, androgynous male models to the catwalk (something we're still seeing today), Slimane brought a skinny-cut jean to fashion as well.

Looking back, the Dior Homme jeans of the early 2000s aren't as skinny as people like to remember, especially in comparison to some of the offerings available today. However, it was what Hedi Slimane did at Dior Homme that ushered in the skinny-fit jeans we're now so accustomed to seeing. It's worth noting that Slimane was supposedly inspired by the cut of the 'New Standard' jeans by A.P.C. (pages 74–7).

Although the Dior Homme name is more familiar to those interested in high fashion than denim, its impact on the world of jeans, especially in regard to style, is up there with some of the original jeans pioneers. And all thanks to Hedi Slimane and his vision for the future of men's fashion.

Opposite: Hedi Slimane's love for London's indie boys brought skinny jeans to the forefront of men's fashion, slimming down the male silhouette.

Dior Homme jeans by Hedi Slimane

2001

Kuyichi jeans

2001

Kuyichi was founded in 2001 as a response to the denim industry's lack of interest in organic cotton. Founded by Dutch NGO Solidaridad, Kuyichi was formed as a way of encouraging the denim industry to use organic cotton by using a lead-by-example strategy.

Today Kuyichi still manufactures high-quality organic denim jeans in a process that is 100 per cent sustainable and responsible, following the original brand ethos. Although the jeans the brand produces may not have had a huge impact on style and the denim market, its pioneering example has. Since the creation of Kuyichi and its organic denim jeans in 2001, a large list of denim brands, from major players such as Nudie Jeans and Howies, to small upstarts such as Hiut Denim, have all begun offering organic denim jeans as part of their collections.

Kuyichi continues to innovate in an attempt to lead the denim industry in the direction it feels it needs to move, currently putting its focus on denim made from recycled cotton, plastic bottles and alternative materials such as hemp and Tencel.

Opposite and below: Through its promotion of organic cotton, Kuyichi has changed the denim industry. Today, many brands use organic denim for some or all of their products.

In 2001 a new Swedish denim brand released its first collection to the world, Nudie Jeans. Having left her position as chief of design at Lee Europe, Maria Erixon started her own brand with a focus on transparency in every part of the manufacturing process. Each different fit of Nudie Jeans received a name inspired by Erixon's friends and family, with this particular style receiving the name 'Regular Ralf'.

The 'Regular Ralf' was a subtle bootcut jean that proved a popular fit in its time, partly thanks to the lingering popularity of both bootcut and loose-fitting baggy jeans. Later on, the 'Regular Ralf' would be renamed the 'Regular Alf', supposedly because of a dispute over the Ralf name with Ralph Lauren. In the face of the dying popularity of bootcut jeans, the 'Regular Alf' would once again change to become the 'Straight Alf' that is available today.

Although it offers a wealth of washes, Nudie Jeans has always specialized in unwashed, dry-selvage denim. The company's arrival in the denim world spearheaded a revival in popularity for dry denim and the craftsmanship involved in the ageing of denim. Nudie not only supplies consumers with high-quality product, but also seeks to educate them on the endless topic of denim.

Today Nudie Jeans is one of the leading denim brands, still maintaining a strong focus on dry denim. Since Fall 2012, all Nudie jeans are manufactured from organic cotton, an achievement of which the brand is rightfully proud.

Opposite: 109
Representing the beginning of the Nudie Jeans brand, the 'Regular Ralf' jean marks an important shift in popular denim culture.

Nudie Jeans 'Regular Ralf'

2001

In 2002 a new name entered the market that would soon become a denim super-brand with its own unique and memorable style – True Religion.

Inspired by the denim of the 1970s, Jeff Lubell began experimenting with sewing techniques to create a product that was different and instantly recognizable. Early offerings used seven different coloured threads – threads that were substantially thicker, too, than anything used on denim before. The 'Big-T' and 'Super-T' were born, their use of two-stitches-per-inch sewing techniques, oversize custom hardware and cowboy-shirt-style button-down back pockets making them very hard to miss.

Thanks to their Made in America high-quality denim and elaborate finishes, True Religion jeans have never been cheap. As with many luxury goods, the high price tag and easy recognition helped True Religion to gain an unexpected but loyal fan base in hip-hop culture. Leading this popularity is the brand's most visually recognizable designs, the 'Big-T' and 'Super-T'.

Opposite and below: The oversized stitching, buttoned back pockets and bold branding made True Religion jeans instantly recognizable.

True Religion 'Big-T' and 'Super-T'

2002

Created by the Japan Blue Group in 2005, Momotaro Jeans is a denim brand focused solely on quality Japanese denim.

The brand took its inspiration and name from the Japanese folklore character Momotaro – a small boy born out of a giant peach who helps his adoptive parents, an elderly couple, to become young again and follow their dreams. It's a fitting reference point for a brand that aimed to encourage the denim industry and the consumer alike to look to the early years of denim culture and aspire to the levels of quality and craftsmanship they were at risk of forgetting.

The Momotaro brand consists of three main labels: Copper, Going to Battle and Vintage. Each takes a slightly different approach, but all use high-quality Zimbabwean cotton that is hand-dyed using natural indigo in Japan then woven on vintage shuttle looms. The jeans are even sewn together on vintage sewing machines, and each stage of the manufacture is done by one of the four Japan Blue Group companies.

Momotaro takes its ideology to an extreme with the more rarely seen Gold Label jeans, each of which is handcrafted with the view of making the perfect pair of jeans, regardless of the cost. These jeans are handmade in Japan from start to finish: the denim is woven on a hand loom and hand-dyed before being cut, sewn and washed once in sea water. Buttons are made from pure silver and the jeans lined with silk. It's a laborious and slow process and, because no corners are cut, some Gold Label Momotaro jeans have commanded retail prices of over $2,000 a pair.

At a time when the people at the Japan Blue Group felt that Japanese consumers were losing their knowledge and appreciation for artisan denim production, it took it upon itself to lead by example. Momotaro is now one of the most highly regarded denim brands in the world.

Opposite and below: Displaying a true love for superior quality denim, the Momotaro brand has gained a loyal following across the globe.

Momotaro Jeans

2005

Workers in the Momotaro Jeans factory in Japan closely inspect rolls of denim during the manufacturing process.

As the trend for slimmer jeans continued to march forwards throughout the 2000s, Nudie Jeans introduced what is now their most popular fit, the 'Thin Finn'.

The 'Thin Finn' was inspired by the carrot jean shape of the 1950s, though to modernize it Nudie made it slimmer and gave it a low back yoke. Washed variations of the 'Thin Finn' are manufactured with stretch denim to reduce the chances of ripping, something that is commonplace in skinny jeans today. It also comes in a dry denim option. Although by today's standards the 'Thin Finn' isn't a drastically skinny jean, at its time of introduction it was a very narrow style. Back then people who weren't ready to commit to the skinny jeans look, but enjoyed the cut of the 'Thin Finn', often wore a size up.

Although never going as far in skinny fit as some brands, Nudie Jeans was an important brand in the progressive slimming of jeans over the last decade.

Opposite and below: Since its arrival in 2005, the slim-fitting 'Thin Finn' has become Nudie's most popular style of jeans.

117

Nudie Jeans 'Thin Finn'

2005

Nudie Jeans
'Lab Joe Nudie Lab 1'

2008

At a time when consumer interest in high-quality denim was growing once again, Nudie Jeans launched its experimental Selvage Lab line. The line was aimed at collectors, with jeans produced in strictly limited editions in its sample lab in Sweden.

As the Nudie Jeans brand continued to grow on a global scale, the Selvage Lab line allowed the brand to continue to experiment. This is where Nudie take its denim geekery to an unrestrained level. The jeans are (almost) all inspired by real vintage and worn-in jeans, often replicated as closely as possible and upgraded in regard to materials and manufacture. One style from the first release in 2008 was actually a raw denim, but since then all pairs have been washed in various different ways. Every pair features silver hardware, slim belt loops and embossed leather patches. All are unique.

Although this sort of vintage replication and attention to detail had been essayed previously by the likes of Levi's Vintage Clothing (see pages 94–7) and Momotaro (see pages 112–13), Nudie took it out of the 'ivory tower' of the denim specialists and put it in front of the more mainstream consumer, thanks to the already well-established Nudie Jeans brand name. Once again, Nudie was educating the masses on denim.

Opposite and below: The Nudie Jeans Selvage Lab produces extremely limited-edition jeans from the Nudie Jeans sample lab.

Junya Watanabe is well known for seeking out the best of the best for his collections with Comme des Garçons Man, preferring to use existing manufacturing experts rather than attempt to replicate or compete. One of those collaborators is Levi's, the forefather of jeans.

Watanabe initially started working with Levi's in his collections for heavy shirting and created his first pair of collaborative jeans with the brand in 2007. Although the Japanese designer was no stranger to putting patches of contrasting materials on his jeans (having done so, for example, in his hunting-inspired jeans for Autumn/Winter 2009), it wasn't until his Autumn/Winter 2011 collection that he truly created his patchwork denim jeans.

While Watanabe certainly didn't create patchwork denim, he is the name most closely associated with it in fashion and is responsible for its recent surge in popularity. Having put it into his Autumn/Winter 2011 collection, it was several years before it gained traction, most likely due to its daring visual aesthetic. In 2013 the Junya Watanabe patchwork jeans by Levi's were a must-have item, at least for those who were brave enough to wear them.

Opposite: A striking look for those with enough style to do them justice, Levi's Junya Watanabe jeans are an homage to the tradition of patching up your own denim.

Levi's Junya Watanabe patchwork jeans

2011

Index

126 Mitchell Beazley would like to acknowledge and thank all those who have kindly provided material for publication in this book.

Page 2 © Walé Adeyemi; 8 © Levi Strauss & Co; 9, 10, 12–13 image courtesy The Advertising Archives; 14-23 © Levi Strauss & Co; 24–6, 34, 35 Courtesy of the Lee Jeans Corporate Archive; 28–32, 36 © Levi Strauss & Co; 38 © Wrangler; 40 Ken Towner/ Associated Newspapers/Rex; 42, 46 Pictorial Press Ltd/Alamy; 44 Warner Bros/The Kobal Collection/McCarty, Floyd; 45 cineclassico/Alamy; 48 Moviestore Collection Ltd/Alamy; 50, 51 © Edwin Jeans; 52, 54, 56–7, 62 © Big John Corporation; 58 Condé Nast Archive/Corbis; 60 The Advertising Archives; 64 Al Freni/The Life Images Collection/Getty Images; 66 DWD-Media/Alamy; 68 AF archive/Alamy; 70 ©Rifle Srl; 72 photo Karl Adamson © Octopus Publishing Group; 74, 76, 77 © END; 78a The Advertising Archives; 78b © Diesel; 80 © EVISU; 82 The Advertising Archives; 84 Barry King/ Wirelmage/Getty Images; 85 Richard Corkery/New York Daily News Archive via Getty Images; 86 Kate Garner/ Corbis; 88 Idols/Photoshot; 90 Scott Wintrow/Getty Images; 92 © ACNE Studios; 94-97 © Levi Strauss & Co; 98 © Big John Corporation; 100 © Michael Benabib/Photoshot; 102, 103 © Walé Adeyemi; 104 Catwalking.com; 106, 107 ©Kuyichi; 108 © Nudie Jeans Co; 110, 111 © True Religion; 112, 113, 114–15 © Momotaro Jeans; 116–19 © Nudie Jeans Co; 120 Martin Bureau/AFP/Getty Images.

Acknowledgements

An Hachette UK Company
www.hachette.co.uk

First published in Great Britain in 2015
by Mitchell Beazley, a division of
Octopus Publishing Group Ltd
Carmelite House
50 Victoria Embankment
London EC4Y 0DZ
www.octopusbooks.co.uk
www.octopusbooksusa.com

Distributed in the US by
Hachette Book Group
1290 Avenue of the Americas
4th and 5th Floors
New York, NY 10020

Distributed in Canada by
Canadian Manda Group
664 Annette St.
Toronto, Ontario, Canada M6S 2C8

ISBN 978 1 84533 996 8

A CIP catalogue record for this book
is available from the British Library

Printed and bound in China

10 9 8 7 6 5 4 3 2 1

Commissioning Editor:
Joe Cottington
Editor:
Alex Stetter
Copy-editor:
Robert Anderson
Art Director:
Jonathan Christie
Design:
Untitled
Picture Researcher:
Nick Wheldon
Assistant Production Manager:
Caroline Alberti

Credits

128 Founded in 2009, The Daily Street is one of the world's leading destinations for up-to-date news, reviews and features on men's fashion and lifestyle, from the biggest stories in streetwear to the latest news in music, art and live events.

Based in London, the TDS team work closely with brands and retailers – from small independent start-ups to global leaders – to bring together a curated edit of happenings in the streetwear world. Whether it's exclusive interviews with key industry names, commissioned videos and photo shoots, exclusive music content or articles covering everything from classic sneakers to news on the very latest releases, The Daily Street is one of the most highly respected voices in streetwear.

www.thedailystreet.co.uk

About the author